Let The Trumpet Sound For Christmas

from Easy to Advanced Levels

PLAYBACK+
Speed • Pitch • Balance • Loop

To access audio visit:
www.halleonard.com/mylibrary

Enter Code
5826-1941-6478-8543

ISBN 978-0-9896705-6-2

Music Minus One

EXCLUSIVELY DISTRIBUTED BY
HAL•LEONARD®

Visit Hal Leonard Online at
www.halleonard.com

Contact us:
Hal Leonard
7777 West Bluemound Road
Milwaukee, WI 53213
Email: info@halleonard.com

In Europe, contact:
Hal Leonard Europe Limited
42 Wigmore Street
Marylebone, London, W1U 2RN
Email: info@halleonardeurope.com

In Australia, contact:
Hal Leonard Australia Pty. Ltd.
4 Lentara Court
Cheltenham, Victoria, 3192 Australia
Email: info@halleonard.com.au

Remembering Christmas past in a Musical Family

Whenever I recall Christmas, images of family gatherings, scrumptious food and MUSIC fill my mind with joyful and nostalgic memories!

There's Dad chopping wood for a fire to roast chestnuts while Mom is busy preparing another amazing meal with a background of Christmas songs from the record player. Mix in extremely boisterous, interactive conversation Italian style and you get the picture!

Nothing terribly unique about this scenario so far, but what transformed it was Mom and Dad were musicians, and inevitably Mom would "appear" at the upright piano with Dad quickly joining her for some live Christmas music. She had a way of creating a "rhythm section" all by herself, and this, combined with an uncanny sense of playing the "right chords" to every song all by "ear," soon became another Christmas family jam!

Dad was the schooled musician, having studied the violin as a young boy with a professor from La Scala Milano. My sister Yvonne played piano and sang, and my brother Glenn, who later reached great accomplishments on both the trumpet and saxophone, even as a tyke sat on the floor and tried to translate what he heard in his mind through Dad's trumpet. (Yes, Dad switched to the trumpet early on finding the violin less suited to his dramatic personality.) This would go on for an hour or so with Mom segueing from one to another song and me playing many of the selections from this Music Minus One volume.

I hope to follow this up with a second volume that will include the lovely Christmas carol "Cantique de Noel" or, as its better known title, "Oh Holy Night." This actually was one of my first trumpet solos with Mom accompanying me. (Yes, she did that also by ear!)

One of my favorites, Mel Torme's "The Christmas Song" or as it's better known, "Chestnuts Roasting On An Open Fire," is included in this volume, and do you know, to this day when I play it during my gigs in the Christmas season, the images and, of course the aroma of Dad roasting chestnuts on an open fire, are right there with me!

Although this album is intended to be a celebration of Christmas music in a play-along format, I heartily recommend that you sing these songs with the minus tracks before playing them. Remember, songs were made to sing! Hey, that's not a bad lyric! No wonder the great Alec Wilder already used it in his gorgeous waltz "While We're Young"!

In other words, use your God-given instrument before you put the horn to your lips. Your goal is to "internalize" these melodies rather than develop your vocal technique. By the way, that's exactly what I did before recording them. In my prior MMO albums, I go into detail on how to develop this natural or ear-based approach to acquiring the art of phrasing and improvisational skills.

Keep this single advice in mind while singing and playing these wonderful songs and you may be pleasantly surprised: Think story, lyrics and emotion and it will act as a GPS of a kind to keep you on track.

Bob Zottola, November 10, 2013, Naples, Florida
Bobzottola@naplesjazzlovers.com

LET THE TRUMPET SOUND FOR CHRISTMAS

CONTENTS

Have Yourself a Merry Little Christmas

Words and Music by
HUGH MARTIN and RALPH BLANE

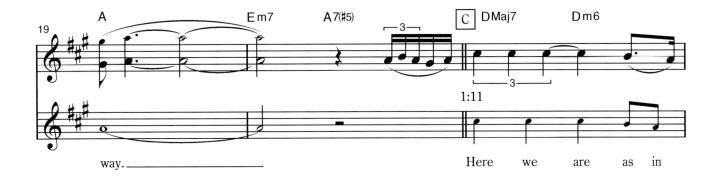

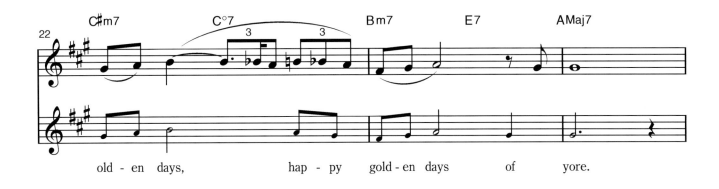

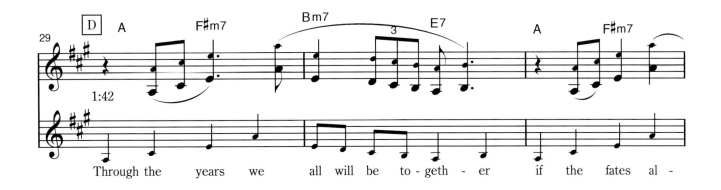

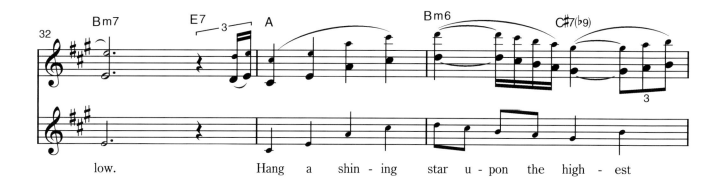

low. Hang a shin - ing star u - pon the high - est

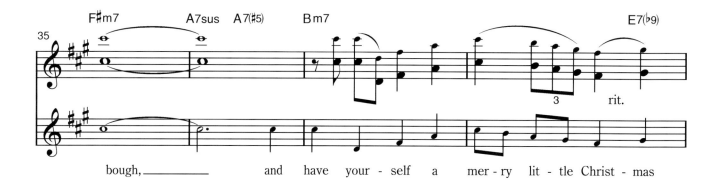

bough,_____ and have your - self a mer - ry lit - tle Christ - mas

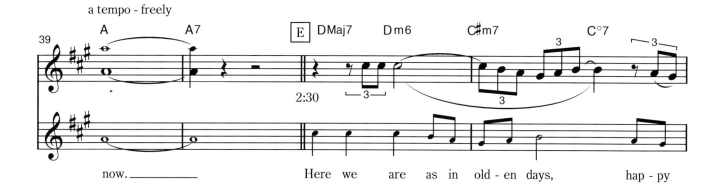

now._____ Here we are as in old - en days, hap - py

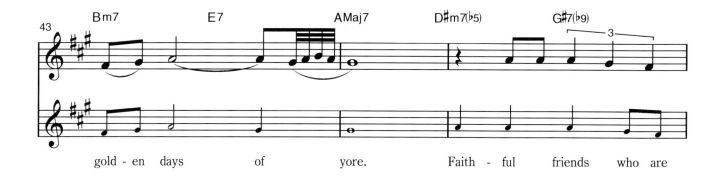

gold - en days of yore. Faith - ful friends who are

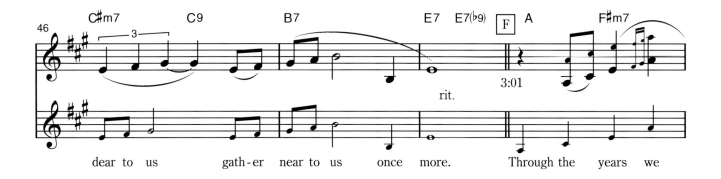

dear to us　　gath-er　near to us　　once more.　　Through the　years　we

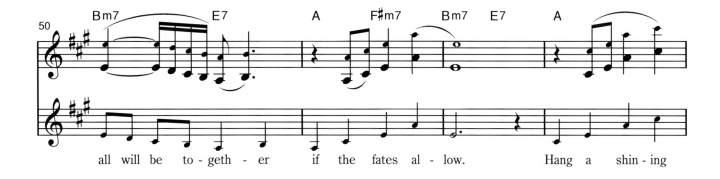

all will be　to-geth-er　if the fates al-low.　　Hang a　shin-ing

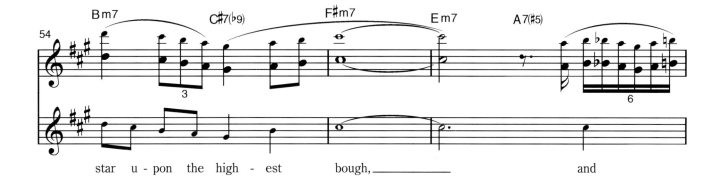

star u-pon the high-est　bough,＿＿＿＿＿　　and

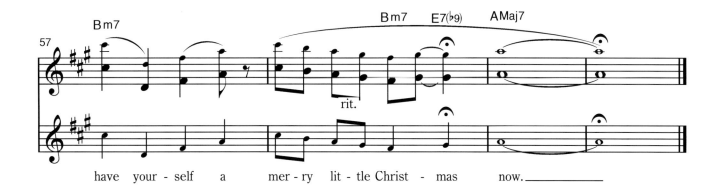

have your-self　a　mer-ry　lit-tle Christ-mas　now.＿＿＿＿

Santa Claus Is Coming to Town

SOLO Bb TRUMPET
FLUGELHORN

Words by Haven Gillespie
Music by J.Fred Coots

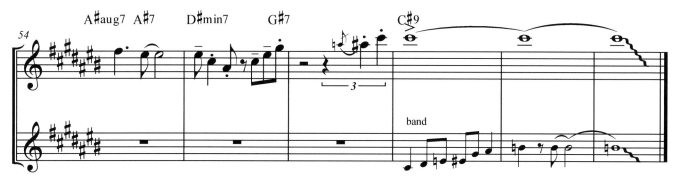

Transcription and engraving by Kevin Mauldin

Silent Night

SOLO Bb TRUMPET
(FLUGELHORN)

Franz Gruber
Josef Mohr

Transcription and engraving by Kevin Mauldin

MMO 6848

I'll Be Home for Christmas

SOLO Bb TRUMPET
FLUGELHORN

Words and Music by
K. Gannon K.Walker
B. Ram

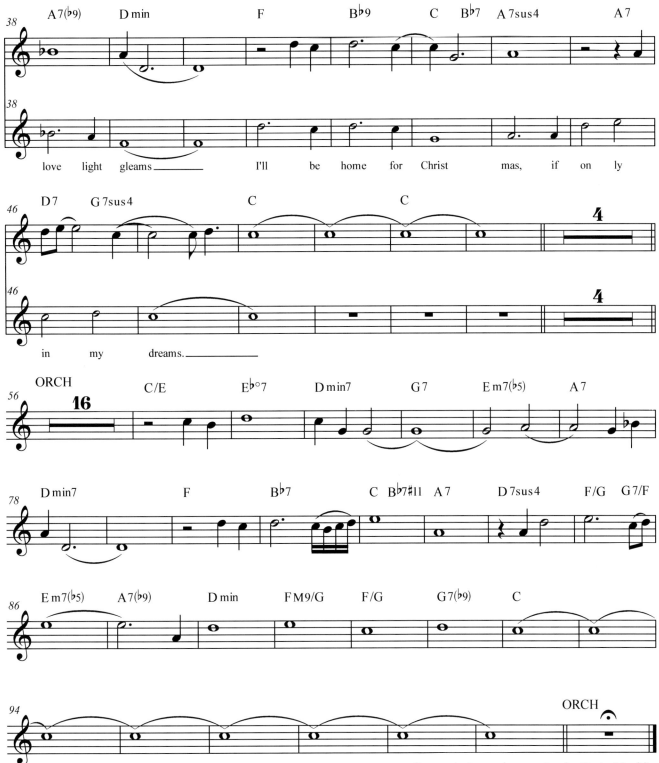

Transcription and engraving by Kevin Mauldin

Count Your Blessings

Irving Berlin

MMO 6848

pic-ture curl-y heads, and one by one I count them as they slum-ber in their

beds. If you're wor-ried and you can't sleep just count your bless-ings in-

stead of sheep and you'll fall a-asleep count-ing your bless - ings

Transcription and engraving by Kevin Mauldin

I've Got My Love to Keep Me Warm

SOLO Bb TRUMPET
(FLUGELHORN)

Irving Berlin

Transcription and engraving by Kevin Mauldin

MMO 6848

White Christmas

Irving Berlin Publishing
The publisher does not permit the reprinting of the music to
White Christmas.

Irving Berlin

Bob's Solo

Transcription and engraving by Kevin Mauldin

SOLO B♭ TRUMPET
(FLUGELHORN)

The Christmas Song

Mel Torme and Robert Wells

MMO 6848

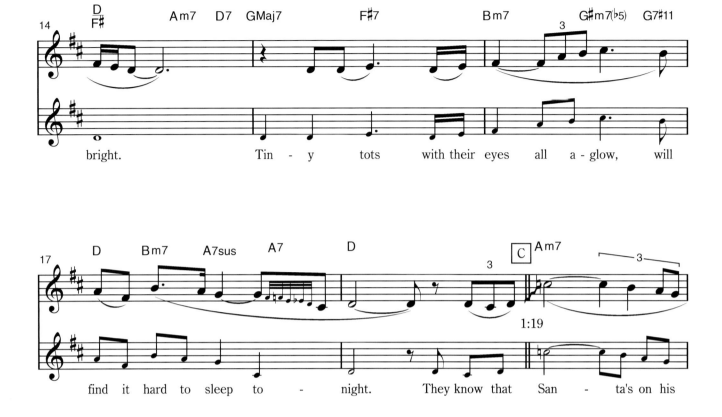

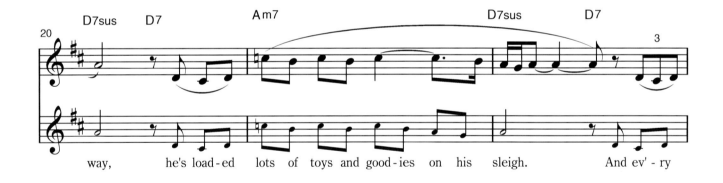

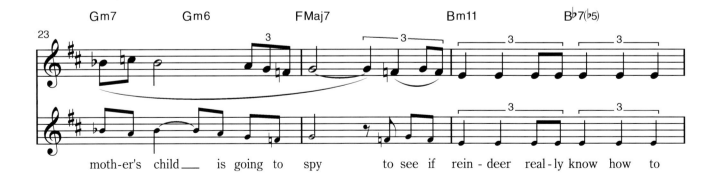

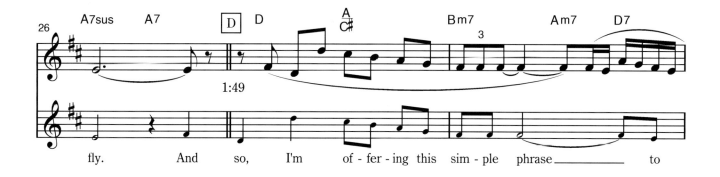

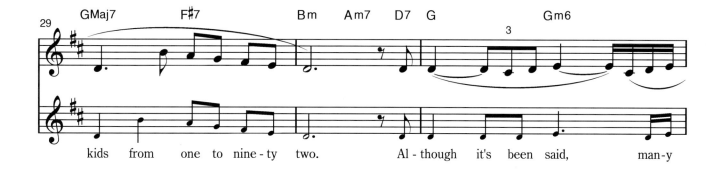

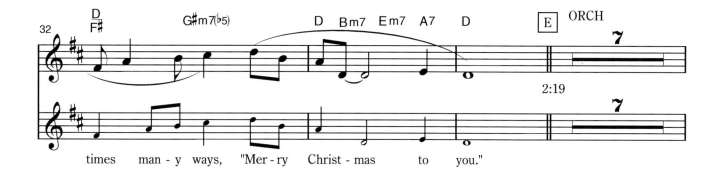

The Christmas Waltz

Jule Styne
Sammy Cahn

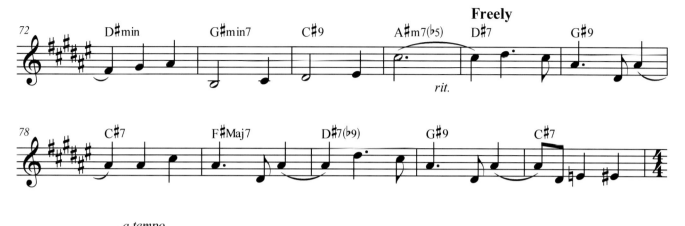

Transcribed and engraved by Kevin Mauldin

What Are You Doing New Year's Eve?

Frank Loesser

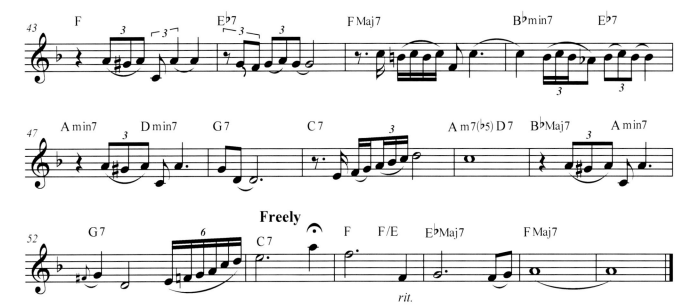

Transcription and engraving by Kevin Mauldin